Donate

* Kitty ☆ ♡ Super Star ♡

Witness History Series

THE USA
SINCE 1945

Nigel Smith

Wayland

Titles in this series

The Arab-Israeli Conflict
China since 1945
The Cold War
The Origins of the First World War
The Russian Revolution
South Africa since 1948
The Third Reich
Towards European Unity
The United Nations

Cover illustration: Astronaut Irwin poses besides the US flag on the moon.

First published in 1989 by
Wayland (Publishers) Limited
61 Western Road, Hove
East Sussex BN3 1JD, England

Editor: Catherine Ellis
Designer: Ross George
Consultant: Chris Gerry, history teacher, and tutorial fellow at Sussex University.

British Library Cataloguing in Publication Data
Smith, Nigel
    The USA since 1945. – (Witness history).
    1. United States, history
    I. Title   II. Series
    973

    ISBN 1–85210–660–3

Typeset by Kalligraphics Limited, Horley, Surrey
Printed and bound by Sagdos, S.p.A., Milan

Contents

1
THE USA COMES OF AGE
An industrial giant

'WE ARE ENTERING A NEW era,' declared Henry Ford in 1920, 'Our new thinking and new doing are bringing us a new world, and a new heaven, and a new earth.'[1] With the First World War behind it and determined to isolate itself from world affairs, the USA entered a period of rapid economic growth that brought widespread prosperity. The mass production of the motor car pioneered by Ford changed the American way of life, and set a model of factory efficiency for other industries. New products, and the companies that made them, became household names throughout the country and the world. The three presidents of the 1920s, Harding, Coolidge and Hoover, were all Republicans and represented the views of business and the Wall Street stock market.

In spite of prohibition, which made all alcoholic drinks illegal, new entertainment industries such as the Hollywood movies, network radio and popular jazz music, brought pleasure to people in every part of the country. Satisfaction with the success of their capitalist private enterprise system made Americans patriotic and firmly opposed to the communist ideas emerging after the 1917 Russian Revolution. 'We are a happy people,' said President Hoover summing it all up; 'We have more cars, more bathtubs, oil furnaces, silk stockings, bank accounts than any other people on earth.'[2] There were few who doubted that Americans had got it right.

The great stock market crash of October 1929 brought an abrupt end to the prosperity. Before the crash unemployment had

Mass production of the Model T Ford on the assembly lines in Detroit changed the appearance of American towns and ushered in a new way of life.

▲ At the peak of the depression nearly one quarter of the workforce were unemployed and charities set up soup kitchens.

been only two million, but by 1933 it had reached fifteen million and industrial production had fallen by 50 per cent. The Great Depression that followed the stock market collapse was a shattering experience. Bankrupt farmers, the jobless in breadlines, the homeless living in tents and the hobos travelling across the country, were a sombre contrast to the booming 1920s.

In 1932 the voters turned to a Democrat, Franklin D. Roosevelt, and his New Deal policies to rescue the economy and to help those suffering the most from unemployment. Roosevelt rallied the nation when he confidently declared at his Inauguration in 1933: 'The only thing we have to fear is fear itself.' He set up agencies to direct the economy, regulate industries and provide welfare, while the Works Progress Administration put millions of people to work on vital projects such as new roads, dams and

▲ President Roosevelt kept in touch with the people through his frequent fireside chats over the radio.

hospitals. By 1940, Roosevelt had helped to reduce unemployment to six million, but even he could not repair all the damage caused by the Depression. Only during the Second World War did unemployment disappear completely, as industries increased production to make the USA the 'arsenal of democracy'.

War and victory

Japan's surprise attack on Pearl Harbor outraged Americans and united them behind the war effort.

For the first two years of the Second World War, American public opinion remained opposed to full US involvement in another European war. The American navy did help to protect British merchant shipping, however, and Axis Consulates in the USA were closed. In August 1941 Roosevelt joined Churchill in issuing the Atlantic Charter which explicitly condemned Nazi tyranny. Then on 7 December 1941, the Sunday afternoon football games and radio broadcasts were interrupted with the shocking news that Japan had mounted a surprise and devastating attack on the US naval base at Pearl Harbor in Hawaii.

There was no hesitation in the USA's reaction to the attack. In his declaration of war on Japan, President Roosevelt described the attack as a 'day of infamy' and promised that, 'the American people in their righteous might will win through to absolute victory.'[3]

Five days after Pearl Harbor, Hitler, in support of his Japanese ally, declared Germany to be at war with the USA.

Before the USA entered the Second World War many Americans had been isolationists, arguing that what happened elsewhere in the world was not the concern of the USA. Others, including President Roosevelt, had always felt strong sympathy for Britain and the other democracies struggling against Nazi Germany. Pearl Harbor ended this conflict of opinion and the nation united behind the war effort.

The USA brought to its allies huge resources of fighting men, and also its great industries capable of producing the weapons and equipment needed for victory. At the height of the war, 12,300,000

Americans were in the armed forces. A total of 291,557 Americans were killed by enemy action, heavier casualties than the British sustained. The financial cost was about $330 billion.

It took four years to achieve the absolute victory Roosevelt had promised. On 6 June 1944, known as D-Day, Allied forces of British, Canadian, French and US troops under the command of US General Dwight D. Eisenhower invaded German-occupied France. Steadily the German forces were driven back, while to the east of Germany the USSR was also pushing Hitler's troops towards Berlin. In spite of being allies, the USA was suspicious of the USSR and keen to prevent too much of Germany falling into its hands.

President Roosevelt died suddenly in 1945, just before the victories over Germany and Japan that he had worked so hard to achieve. Part of Roosevelt's legacy was the United Nations, which he helped to set up during the last years of the war. Its major aim was to preserve world peace, helping countries to resolve problems through negotiation rather than war. The Second World War established the USA as the leading power in the West with a commitment to playing a major role in world affairs. At the end of the Second World War, the USSR was seeking to create satellite Soviet states in Eastern Europe and the USA was in possession of the atomic bomb; the world was moving into the dangerous new era of the cold war and the atomic age.

7 June 1944, Americans land on a beach in northern France. The D-Day invasion by the allies marked the beginning of the liberation of Europe.

2
THE FAIR DEAL
President Truman 1945–52

HARRY TRUMAN HAD BEEN vice-president for only eighty-three days when, on the 12 April 1945, the sudden death of President Roosevelt precipitated him into the presidency. The Second World War was drawing to a close. It was at his first Cabinet meeting that the new president learned of the existence of the atomic bomb, and in early August 1945 he took the grim decision to authorize its use against the Japanese cities of Hiroshima and Nagasaki in an attempt to force Japan to accept defeat. The

devastation caused by the atomic bomb had the desired effect, and on 14 August Truman announced Japan's surrender.

Hopes for permanent peace were focused on the United Nations, and within minutes of taking office President Truman had pledged the USA's commitment to this new international organization. It was not long, however, before the wartime allies, the USSR and the USA, fell out. In fact, the Truman presidency was dominated by continual tension between the two nations; in the background was the knowledge that another world war would probably involve the use of atomic weapons that had the capacity to destroy humankind.

The awful wartime experience of invasion by the Germans made the USSR fear for its future security. In the West, the USA perceived Soviet intentions as aggressive and threatening. The mutual fear and suspicion that developed between the two became known as the cold war. Truman was determined to contain the Soviets, and in 1949 the Western powers formed a military alliance, the North Atlantic Treaty Organization (NATO). The USSR accused the USA of failing to understand its need for security and creating the cold war tension.

Truman was never as popular as Roosevelt had been, but he became a tough speaker and earned respect as a gutsy politician. When his Republican opponents complained that he was giving them 'hell', he replied, 'I don't give 'em hell, I just tell the truth and they think it's hell.'[4] The slogan on his White House desk read, 'The buck stops here'. In November 1948, even though the opinion polls were unanimous in predicting his defeat, Truman dumbfounded his critics and even his supporters by winning re-election.

The news of President Roosevelt's sudden death, shortly before the end of the Second World War, was received with shock and sadness.

◄ In 1945 only the USA possessed the atomic bomb, and its existence was a major influence on post-war foreign policy.

▼ Harry Truman was not well-known when he unexpectedly had to take over as president on the death of Roosevelt.

Truman's presidency was overshadowed by the cold war, and by war in Korea. However, his domestic policies, known as the Fair Deal, reflected post-war idealism with plans for national health insurance and action to improve the civil rights of black Americans. On both of these the more conservative Congress defeated him, but as Commander-in-Chief of the armed services Truman was able to end the segregation that kept black and white servicemen separate in the armed forces.

The cold war

The Marshall Plan helped to rebuild post-war Europe by supplying much-needed equipment. Why was the USA keen to assist Europe?

Following the defeat of Germany in 1945, various east European countries came under Soviet domination, and Germany itself was divided into zones of occupation by the four Allies. Germany's former capital, Berlin, was also split among the Allies into four zones and occupied by British, French, American and Soviet troops. The entire city, however, was contained within the Soviet zone of East Germany, and on several occasions Berlin was the focus of tension between the USSR and the West.

The shattered economies and political chaos in many countries at the end of the war provided ideal conditions for the spread of communism. The USA was determined to halt Soviet expansion. At the heart of the argument was the conflict between two very different political and economic systems. In 1947 a State Department official declared:

> *United States policy toward the Soviet Union must be that of a long-term, patient but firm and vigilant containment of Russian expansive tendencies.*[5]

Why did the USA feel so threatened by any increase in the influence of the USSR in Europe? The USSR and USA had fought together during the war, so why could they not continue to be on good terms after the war?

In 1947 the Truman Doctrine set out the USA's tough line:

> *...it must be the policy of the United States to support free people who are resisting attempted subjugation by armed minorities or by outside pressures . . . our help should be primarily through economic and financial aid which is essential to economic stability and political processes.*[6]

The Truman Doctrine made it clear that the USA would be actively involved in the internal affairs of other countries in order to stop the spread of communism. However, not all the people in the countries that Truman had in mind welcomed the American involvement. Why might they oppose American 'assistance'? One result of the Truman Doctrine was that the USA sometimes, as in Greece in 1947, supported repressive or corrupt politicians simply because they were anti-communist.

In June 1947, the secretary of state, George Marshall, announced the European Recovery Program or Marshall Plan:

The recovery of Europe has been far slower than had been expected. Disintegrating forces are becoming evident. The patient is sinking while the doctors deliberate . . .[7]

The Marshall Plan provided $12.5 billion to sixteen nations and reduced the likelihood of vulnerable countries choosing communist governments. The USSR complained of American arrogance. To what extent was the USA entitled to interfere in the affairs of other nations? Certainly the policy sharpened the division between the USSR and the USA, and we must ask how far Truman's policy was responsible for heightening the cold war.

British and American planes broke the 1948-49 Soviet blockade of West Berlin.

The Korean War

◀ MacArthur's approach to the Korean War was more popular than the president's, and many people were angry when Truman sacked him.

This cable was sent by the US Embassy in Seoul on 25 June 1950:

> *North Korean forces invaded Republic of Korea territory at several places this morning.*[8]

At the end of the Second World War, Korea had been divided in two, the North under communist rule, the South supported by the USA. When the North Koreans invaded in 1950, President Truman ordered in troops to oppose them. He was determined to show that the USA would use its military muscle to back up its commitment to the Truman Doctrine.

> *The attack upon Korea makes it plain beyond all doubt that communism has passed beyond the use of subversion to conquer independent nations and will now use armed invasion and war.*[9]

However, Truman's conduct of the war was controversial. General MacArthur, US commander in Korea, argued for a total commitment to achieving a military victory. He supported the idea of pushing up through North Korea and into China:

> *If we lose the war to communism in Asia, the fall of Europe is inevitable; win it and Europe most probably would avoid war and yet preserve freedom . . . There is no substitute for victory.*[10]

Truman's problem was trying to win the war in Korea without it escalating into a major conflict with China or the USSR, which MacArthur's command threatened. Truman could not risk an extension of the fighting, so in 1953 he sought an armistice. The president felt compelled to sack MacArthur, a move that was received with a storm of protest. Why did so many Americans support MacArthur? It was difficult for them to understand Truman's concern to avoid direct conflict with China and the USSR. Public opinion turned against Truman.

Gallup opinion poll[11]
July 1951

Do you approve or disapprove of the way Harry Truman is handling his job as president?

Approve	25%
Disapprove	59%
No opinion	16%

Chongjin

Chosan

CHINA

USSR

Chinese intervention Oct. 1950

U S maximum advance 24 Nov. 1950

U S task force 77

NORTH KOREA

armistice line 27 July 1953

38° N

38th Parallel

Panmunjom
Seoul

landing of U S X Corps 15 Sept. 1950

Chinese and North Korean maximum advance 25 Jan. 1951

Wonju

SOUTH KOREA

North Korean maximum advance 15 Sept. 1950

Pohang

Taego

Pusan

JAPAN

◄China's proximity to Korea enabled it to give massive support to the North Koreans. Truman's fear was that the USA would be drawn into war with China and the USSR.

▼ Exhausted soldiers sprawl in the mountainous Korean terrain during a lull in the action. One stands guard over their 155mm Howitzer.

Eventually an armistice was signed and the border between North and South Korea returned to the position it was before the invasion. But it had been a costly war for the USA, with 54,000 men killed and over 100,000 wounded. Many Americans were disappointed at the high cost and lack of a decisive victory.

Gallup opinion poll[12]
July 1951

Do you think the United States made a mistake in going into the war in Korea or not?

Yes	51%
No	35%
No opinion	14%

Why was there so much disillusionment? Were Americans critical because they had failed to destroy communist North Korea? Were there any lessons for the future that might have been learned from their involvement in the Korean War?

3
UNEASE AND AFFLUENCE
The Eisenhower years 1952–60

GENERAL DWIGHT D. EISENHOWER served as commander of the Allied forces in Europe during the Second World War. He was a popular choice for the Republican Party as their presidential candidate, and won an easy victory in the 1952 election. Millions of Americans admired Eisenhower as the kind of man who represented the best in their country. He had a frank and open manner and was quick to smile. 'I like Ike' proved an irresistable slogan and, in spite of two heart attacks, he was re-elected in 1956 for a second term.

For many Americans the 1950s was a period of increasing affluence. As more people enjoyed luxury cars, televisions and new suburban homes, their main fear appeared to be of a supposed communist threat to their way of life. Black Americans,

however, were less contented with their way of life. They were increasingly frustrated at the failure to stop discrimination against them; the system of segregation in the southern states subjected them to humiliating discrimination in jobs, housing, education and even the right to vote. At first Eisenhower was reluctant to act, but as the protests grew he finally insisted that the law be enforced to give all citizens their civil rights. The enforcement of equal treatment proved difficult, however, and it has remained an important political issue.

The most spectacular controversy of Eisenhower's presidency was the rise and fall of Joe McCarthy. Senator McCarthy exploited the fear Americans had of the spread of communism. He made wild allegations about widespread communist

▶ A few Americans were so worried by the possibility of a Soviet attack that they built their own private fallout shelters.

▼ Eisenhower's election-winning slogan reflected his wide appeal.

Eisenhower sometimes seemed slow to tackle major problems, but he remained popular.

influence in the government, the press and even in the Hollywood entertainment industry. Although his claims were discredited, many people remained deeply uneasy over the issue of communism.

The main outlet for Americans' dread of communism was in fearing the spread of Soviet and Chinese influence abroad, and there was particular concern that Chinese communists might gain control of countries in South-East Asia. President Eisenhower warned that if one country fell to the communists then the others would follow, like a row of dominoes. His administration poured millions of dollars into countries such as Laos and Vietnam to counter communist attempts to take them over.

Looking to Europe, the Americans worried that in the event of a conflict the Soviet army would be too strong to beat. In 1954, the Secretary of State, John Foster Dulles, declared that the USA must rely on the 'deterrent of massive retaliatory power'.[13] The Americans believed that only their nuclear weapons would stop Soviet aggression, and so an arms race developed as the USSR and USA both strove for nuclear superiority.

In 1957 American self-confidence suffered a blow when the USSR launched the first two spacecraft into orbit. If the Soviets could do this then they could certainly launch nuclear missiles. 'Rocket fever' swept the country and the public demanded of Eisenhower that the missile gap be closed.

McCarthyism

One major political problem in the 1950s was the power and menace of Senator Joe McCarthy. Starting in 1950, he unleashed a series of attacks on many individuals, claiming that they were communists. Although there was no real threat to the American way of life from the Communist Party, many people were uneasy simply because of the spread of Soviet and communist influence abroad. These fears were increased when Klaus Fuchs, a British scientist, confessed to supplying atomic bomb secrets to the USSR and implicated four American citizens. Two of them, Ethel and Julius Rosenberg, were executed for espionage in 1953. McCarthy saw political advantage in exploiting the strong anti-communist mood of the time. There was no truth in McCarthy's allegations, but in the cold war atmosphere many people believed his smears. His claims received massive publicity and he gained a large personal following.

Witch-hunts followed his allegations, and the careers of countless writers, teachers, actors and government officials were ruined by the slur of being named a communist by McCarthy. Politicians were reluctant to oppose him, and even President Eisenhower refused to stand up to him, saying, 'I will not get in the gutter with that guy.'[14]

McCarthy claimed that the government itself contained communists, and that he had a list of 205 members of the Communist Party in the State Department. It was a sensational charge, but quite untrue. McCarthy had created a campaign simply to boost his own political stature. A committee investigated the accusation but found no evidence to support it. However, the damage had been done. McCarthy pressed on with further dramatic claims. Why do you think so many Americans were prepared to believe McCarthy in spite of the lack of evidence? Can you think of any reasons that might have encouraged him to press on with his claims? Imagine how those attacked by

Between 1950 and his death in 1957 Joe McCarthy became the most notorious member of the United States Senate.

McCarthy must have felt. Why was it difficult for them to defend themselves?

There seemed no stopping McCarthy. 'The Senate', said one newspaper, 'is afraid of him.'[15] Why were politicians, including the president, frightened of publicly criticizing him? In 1954 he began to attack officers in the US Army:

Certain individuals in the Army have been protecting, covering up, and honorably discharging known communists . . . If a stupid, arrogant or witless man in a position of power is found aiding the Communist Party he will be exposed.[16]

This time, however, McCarthy had gone too far, as a commentator on NBC Radio noted:

> McCarthy has too often hit below the belt . . . McCarthy uses the same bludgeon to hit an honorable Army general that he swings at a treacherous Communist.[17]

Consider some reasons why it was a mistake for McCarthy to allege the army was concealing communists.

A Senate sub-committee met to study McCarthy's charges. Its hearings were watched by millions on television and gradually public opinion began to turn against him.

> This is no time for men who oppose Senator McCarthy's methods to keep silent, or for some who approve. We proclaim ourselves the defenders of freedom, what's left of it, but we cannot defend freedom abroad by deserting it at home. The actions of the junior senator from Wisconsin have caused alarm and dismay.[18]

The hearings exposed McCarthy's behaviour and irresponsibility to the scrutiny of television audiences and totally discredited him. Why do you think that television coverage destroyed McCarthy?

The term 'McCarthyism' has remained to describe an unfair and untrue attack intended to discredit people who have done nothing wrong. Why was McCarthyism dangerous to the American political system?

Film stars, including Humphrey Bogart, Lauren Bacall, and Danny Kaye, flew to Washington in 1948 to oppose the witch-hunts that attacked many innocent people.

The battle against segregation

Armed troops escort black students into school.

Deep-rooted racial discrimination was normal in the southern states that had once formed the Confederacy. For decades black Americans had suffered appalling discrimination, while white citizens groups fought uncompromisingly to maintain their segregated way of life. Blacks endured constant humiliation as second class citizens. Segregation in schools was the hottest issue.

The nation was deeply divided. In outlawing segregation the Supreme Court said:

Segregation of white and colored children in public schools has a detrimental effect upon the colored children . . . Segregation has a tendency to retard the educational and mental development of Negro children . . .[20]

Consider the impact of this judgement on the southern states.

With the connivance of the authorities, southern whites struggled to stop desegregation. Serious conflict at Little Rock, a High School in Arkansas, in 1957 compelled President Eisenhower to send in troops. He explained the need for soldiers:

This morning the mob again gathered in front of the Central High School, obviously for the purpose of preventing the carrying out of the Court's order relating to the admission of Negro children to that school . . . Mob rule cannot be allowed to override the decisions of our courts.[21]

The New York Times.

PRESIDENT SENDS TROOPS TO LITTLE ROCK,
FEDERALIZES ARKANSAS NATIONAL GUARD;
TELLS NATION HE ACTED TO AVOID ANARCHY

Why was it necessary to send 1,000 soldiers to the Little Rock High School? Why were feelings running so strong? How did it affect the USA's image abroad? Eisenhower had no doubts:

At a time when we face grave situations abroad because of the hatred that communism bears . . . it would be difficult to exaggerate the harm to the prestige and influence of our nation.[22]

What criticism do you think the Soviets made of the USA after events at Little Rock?

Schools were gradually and painfully desegregated, and although prejudice could not be legislated away, the demand for equal civil rights by black Americans gained new momentum and confidence.

◀People were shocked and the nation was split by news of the events at Little Rock. In 1954, twenty states as well as Washington DC had segregated schools (see below).

Segregation required

Local option on segregation

Segregation prohibited

No specific legislation

Confederate states

The affluent society

During the 1950s, Americans enjoyed unprecedented prosperity as a post-war economic boom made theirs the first affluent society. Some items previously thought of as luxuries became accepted as necessities. Sales of televisions, cars, dishwashers and new suburban homes soared. Movies and magazines carried the news of American success to millions of envious people around the world. Vast supermarkets, new freeways, large cars with fins and chrome, and television game shows were all symbols of a flourishing economy.

What do the following statistics suggest about life in the 1950s?

	1950	1960
US home owners (millions)	23.6	32.8
Hot dog sales (millions lbs)	750	1050
Power mower sales (millions)	1	3.8
Washing machine sales (millions)	1.7	2.6
Gin production (millions of gallons)	6	19
Aspirin sales (millions of lbs)	12	18[23]

American prosperity was the envy of the world, but not everyone was able to enjoy the luxuries they saw advertised in magazines and on television.

1. Steel construction; easy-gliding drawers, positive-closing doors. Baked-on enamel finish wipes clean easily!

2. Ample, accessible storage (including corner cabinet with shelves that turn, and rolling-door cabinet for spices)!

3. New Youngstown Kitchens Jet-Tower Dishwasher does dishes in less than 10 minutes!

4. One-piece, acid-resisting porcelain-enameled steel sink top with no-splash bowl.

5. Youngstown Kitchens Food Waste Disposer, 3 ways best, fits Electric or Cabinet Sink, abolishes garbage!

See for yourself!
All you want in your dream kitchen IS HERE!

SEE FOR YOURSELF how new beauty, unheard-of work savings, and lasting value are yours in Youngstown Kitchens.

Imagine a kitchen of long-lasting STEEL; baked-on enamel finishes that wipe clean easily; doors that won't buckle, drawers that won't stick.

Imagine a kitchen that does your dishes the exclusive Jet-Tower way that no man, woman, or other machine can equal . . . a kitchen that eliminates garbage forever . . . creates more accessible storage than you believed possible.

Imagine exactly the kitchen you want in sturdy steel, built to last a housetime — then ask to see it for yourself.

Let your factory-trained Youngstown Kitchen dealer show you your dream kitchen in perfect miniature, show you how to save on installation and how easy it is to finance. If building, specify a Youngstown Kitchen. You'll save!

MULLINS MANUFACTURING CORPORATION WARREN, OHIO
Youngstown Kitchens are sold throughout the World

Youngstown Kitchens

Call Western Union, Operator 25, and without charge get the name of a nearby dealer.

Mullins Manufacturing Corporation
Dept. NG-132, Warren, Ohio
Send 24-page planning and decorating idea book. I enclose 10c for mailing. (No stamps, please.)
I plan to build ☐   I plan to remodel ☐

NAME (Please print)
ADDRESS
CITY   ZONE
COUNTY   STATE

© 1952 Mullins Manufacturing Corporation

See for yourself! Youngstown Kitchens Jet-Tower Dishwasher . . . 58 swirling, booster-heated jets shear under dirt, get dishes hygienically clean in less than ten minutes.

Youngstown Kitchens Food Waste Disposer. Nonstop feeding, double-action shredding, self-cleaning action.

Elvis Presley was one of the new youth heroes that parents deplored.

There was, however, a discordant note. Consider these statistics:

Average personal income 1959

Connecticut	$2817
New York	$2736
California	$2661
South Dakota	$1476
Mississippi	$1162[24]

Find these states on the map on page 19. What do these figures tell us about the distribution of affluence? Can you think of some reasons why people in southern states such as Mississippi might be less well off than those in the north?

In spite of the obvious signs of prosperity, there was also deep and permanent poverty. The government lagged behind European countries in the provision of social welfare. What did John Galbraith, an American economist, mean by the statement: 'In an atmosphere of private opulence and public squalor, the private goods have full sway.'[25]? 'What's good for General Motors,'

said one Cabinet Member, 'is good for the country.' But was that necessarily true? Despite a booming economy, the Congress defeated attempts to set up a national health service. Michael Harrington, a political writer, has pointed out the contradictions in American society regarding poverty:

America has the best dressed poverty the world has ever known . . . It is much easier in the United States to be decently dressed than it is to be decently housed, fed or doctored.[26]

Were middle-class Americans unaware of the problem of poverty, or simply unwilling to support and pay for programmes to tackle it? Do you see any contradiction between the failure of the government to provide decent health care and the politicians who spoke of the need for freedom and justice in other areas of the world?

4
THE NEW FRONTIER
President Kennedy 1961–63

IN 1960, JOHN KENNEDY, a Democrat, defeated his rival Richard Nixon to become president by a margin of only 114,000 out of 68 million votes cast. In spite of his narrow victory he soon enjoyed considerable support. With his wife Jackie and two young children the new First Family caught the imagination of the country. The White House was nicknamed Camelot, after the legendary court of King Arthur, as Kennedy drew in some of the brightest, most talented people· to serve in his administration. Unquestionably Kennedy had style and character, and young Americans in particular were inspired by his articulate and passionate commitment to ideals of freedom and civil rights.

Kennedy's inaugural address set out his view of the New Frontier and he declared that, 'the torch has been passed to a new generation of Americans.' One of the closing passages guaranteed it would evoke a strong response from idealists seeking leadership: 'And so,' he said, 'my fellow Americans, ask not what your country can do for you; ask what you can do for your country.'[27] He established the Peace Corps, as an alternative to military service that enabled young people to help underdeveloped nations. It was not simply idealism or generosity that motivated Kennedy in this, but the chance to win over those nations and halt the spread of communism.

Kennedy's greatest challenges were in foreign affairs. The fiasco of an attempted American invasion of pro-communist Cuba in 1961 – known as the Bay of Pigs – badly damaged his standing. But his tough defence of West Berlin and success in the Cuban missile crisis impressed the world.

The style and glamour of John and Jacqueline Kennedy and their children helped to make them so popular as the nation's First Family.

As they fought it out on television, Kennedy's success in debates with Nixon demonstrated the importance of television in elections.

On the domestic front Kennedy spoke out in support of civil rights, health care and other social programmes, and he was determined that the USA would beat the USSR to the moon. Initially Kennedy was a fairly cautious president, however. Aware of his small electoral majority, his rhetoric tended to outweigh actual legislation. In 1963 Kennedy's presidency was brutally cut short by his assassination, and all his plans were left to his successors to see through.

Historians debate the significance of Kennedy's administration and the direction it would have taken had he lived. Would he, for example, have led the USA into the quagmire of the Vietnam War? His advocates say no, but President Kennedy also has his critics who question the substance of his achievements. His private life has also been criticized. The tragedy of his death makes dispassionate analysis difficult. Ted Sorensen, a close colleague, wrote that Kennedy's greatest contribution was that as president he stood: 'for hope in an era of doubt – for reconciliation between East and West, black and white, labour and management.'[28]

Confrontation in Berlin

The Berlin Wall created new tension in Germany. Kennedy went to see it for himself, and to show support for West Berliners.

Since the end of the Second World War, when Germany was occupied and divided into zones by the allies, Berlin has been a constant cause of friction between the USSR and the USA. Although a part of West Germany, West Berlin can only be reached by passing through communist East Germany. East-West relations deteriorated during the 1950s, and the West refused to officially recognize the East German state. West Berlin's prosperity was in sharp contrast to the dismal conditions in East Germany, and Berlin provided an easy escape route for thousands fleeing from the East. The situation infuriated the East German authorities and was very damaging to their economy. The objective of the USSR was to incorporate the whole of Berlin into East Germany, but some West Germans continued to hope that one day Berlin would again be the capital of a united non-communist Germany.

American policy on Berlin was clear:

1 To maintain the freedom of the people of West Berlin to choose their own political and social system.
2 To keep Western troops in Berlin so long as the people wanted them to remain.
3 To ensure uninterrupted access to the city through East Germany.

The Soviet leader, Khrushchev, was determined to 'eradicate this splinter from the heart of Europe.'[29] What did he mean by a 'splinter', and why was the USSR so determined to have the entire city? What do you think was the strategic importance of Berlin to both sides? Khrushchev repeatedly threatened to hand over control of the Soviet sector of the city to the East Germans. The USA believed that the East Germans would be more difficult to deal with. East Germany was anxious to halt the flood of refugees escaping to the West. President Kennedy had to consider whether it was worth risking a war to defend it. The Soviets were not certain that the USA would actually go to war over West Berlin. By a policy of confrontation they could test American resolve.

Constantly the USSR applied pressure. Kennedy did not want to overreact by threatening war, but he would not respond in any way that could appear weak. He ordered more combat troops into Berlin. Khrushchev regarded this as belligerent:

> We decided to accept the challenge which Kennedy had issued . . . and we built up our own garrison accordingly. We had picked up the gauntlet and were ready for the duel.[30]

Considering the aims of the USSR and the position of Berlin, was Khrushchev justified in accusing the USA of creating a crisis?

In August 1961 the Soviets and East Germans erected the Berlin Wall, completely separating East and West Berlin. Soviet soldiers harassed US patrols at Checkpoint Charlie and other border crossing points, and this provocation intensified the crisis. 'The wall,' said President Kennedy, 'is an offence against humanity, separating families, dividing husbands and wives and brothers and sisters and dividing a people who wish to be joined together.'[31] Kennedy sent 60 armoured trucks carrying 1,500 soldiers along the autobahn to Berlin, and Vice-President Johnson flew in to support the people of West Berlin. It was a demonstration of their commitment. By the end of 1961 the worst of the crisis had passed, although tension remained.

West Berlin is marooned in East Germany.

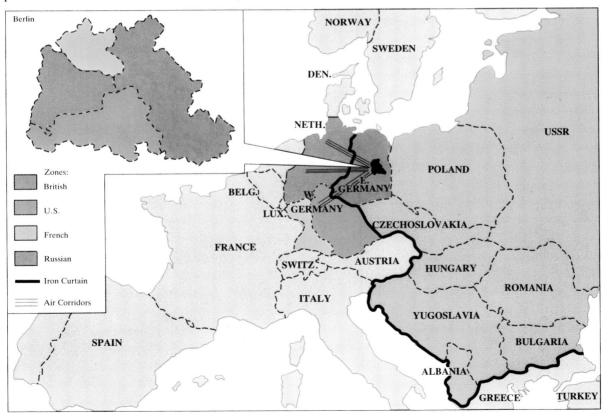

Into space

Nowhere was competition between the USA and the USSR more intense than in space. It was not simply a matter of national prestige but also of military necessity. The Soviets' success in launching a satellite in 1957 showed they had the ability to launch missiles against American cities. The public were upset and alarmed that the Soviets seemed to be more successful than they were in space.

The 1958 Congressional Act setting up the space programme gave three reasons for going into space:
1 National security.
2 Keeping the USA on the leading edge of technology.
3 The determination to use space activities for peaceful and scientific purposes for the benefit of all humankind.[32]

In April 1961 the USSR succeeded in putting the first man into space. The following month President Kennedy responded in a message to Congress:

> *I believe that this nation should commit itself to achieving the goal, before this decade is out, of landing a man on the moon and returning him safely to the earth. No single space project in this period will be more impressive to mankind . . . and none will be so difficult or expensive to accomplish.*[33]

Why do you think President Kennedy set the target of a man on the moon before 1970? To achieve it would be expensive – $25,000 million – and technically very difficult. Might that money have been put to better use? Every space effort was challenged by protests about the very high costs involved, but the president was clearly determined to beat the USSR to the moon because to do so would demonstrate American superiority in technology and science. Did this warrant the enormous expense?

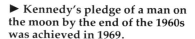

▶ Kennedy's pledge of a man on the moon by the end of the 1960s was achieved in 1969.

◀ The USA was upset and alarmed when the USSR beat them into space, with the launch of this first satellite.

On 21 July 1969, twenty US manned space-flights later, Neil Armstrong set foot on the moon, with the now famous words: 'That's one small step for man – one giant leap for mankind.' He planted a United States flag on the moon, which NASA commented on as follows:

The planting of the flag is symbolic of the first time man has landed on another celestial body and does not constitute a territorial claim by the United States.[34]

Some people had urged that a United Nations flag, to represent humankind, be planted rather than the Stars and Stripes. A month earlier President Nixon had said:

When the first man stands on the moon next month, every American will stand taller because of what he has done, and we should be proud of this achievement.[35]

It seems clear that national pride was a major incentive behind the US space programme.

The Cuban missile crisis

On 16 October 1962 the CIA briefed President Kennedy that Soviet missiles were being installed in Cuba, just a few miles from the coast of Florida. In the photographic evidence below (similar to that which was presented to the president), the Soviet equipment is clearly visible. Within minutes of these missiles being launched eighty million Americans in the eastern half of the USA could have been dead.

Why did the USSR install the missiles? The Soviet leader, Khrushchev, declared:

> *The installation of our missiles in Cuba would, I thought, restrain the United States from precipitous military action against Castro . . . our aim was only to deter America from starting a war.*[36]

Consider the options available to President Kennedy:

1 To do nothing other than protest to the USSR.
2 To seek the assistance of the United Nations in which the USSR has the power of veto.
3 To blockade Cuba to stop any further installation of missiles.
4 To invade Cuba and knock out the Soviet missiles.

Presidential Proclamation 3504 declared:

> *Now, therefore I, John F. Kennedy, President of the United States of America, to defend the security of the United States, do hereby proclaim that the forces under my command are ordered to interdict the delivery of offensive weapons to Cuba.*[37]

What were the merits of a blockade? If the USSR tried to break it then war could result, and if they did not remove the missiles then

Soviet missile equipment can be seen on Cuba in this photograph taken from a US spy plane in October 1962.

CHERRY PICKER

LAUNCH PAD WITH ERECTOR

LAUNCH PAD WITH ERECTOR

MISSILE READY BLDGS

CABLING

OXIDIZER VEHICLES

FUELING VEHICLES

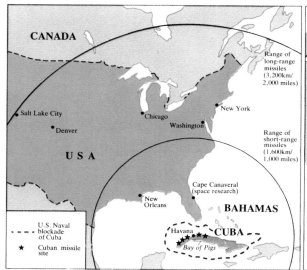

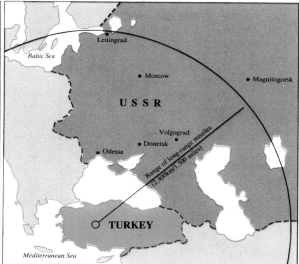

▲ Compare the potential threat of Soviet missiles in Cuba, to the threat of US missiles already installed in Turkey.

◄ There was great tension all over the world as President Kennedy imposed a naval blockade on Cuba to stop Soviet ships carrying missile equipment.

the possibility of an invasion remained. Neither side could afford the humiliation of retreat from the positions they had adopted. President Kennedy told the nation:

> *My fellow citizens: let no one doubt that this is a difficult and dangerous effort on which we have set out . . . But the greatest danger of all would be to do nothing.*[38]

What did he mean by saying it would have been dangerous to have done nothing?

Khrushchev worried that the crisis would escalate beyond either his or the president's control: 'if indeed war should break out, then it would not be in our power to stop it.'[39] The agreement that resolved the crisis presented Kennedy as a hero to his nation and Khrushchev as a conciliatory statesman to his people. The USSR agreed to remove the missiles in return for an American promise not to infringe the sovereignty of Cuba. The question remains, what action would Kennedy have taken if the Soviets had not agreed to withdraw their missiles?

Kennedy's assassination

There was enormous grief and shock when Kennedy was assassinated in the centre of Dallas.

Only 13 per cent of Americans believe the official version of the assassination of President Kennedy on 22 November 1963. They have never entirely come to terms with the shocking murder of their young and popular president. John Kennedy and his wife were riding in a motorcade through Dallas, Texas. Merriman Smith, a reporter, described the shooting:

> Suddenly we heard the loud cracks. The first sounded as if it might have been a firecracker. But the second and third blasts were unmistakeable. Gunfire.[40]

Using the codename of the president, the Secret Service flashed out a desperate message:

> Lancer is hurt. It looks bad. We have got to get to a hospital.[41]

But the wound was fatal, and at Parkland Hospital the White House assistant press secretary announced the death of the president:

> He died of a gunshot wound in the brain. Mrs Kennedy was not hit. Governor Connally (of Texas) was hit. The vice-president was not hit.[42]

Radio and television flashed the news around the world. Consider the reaction of ordinary people as they heard the news. The telephone system became jammed as people tried to call family and friends to tell them the news. How, they asked, could the president be gunned down in broad daylight? Why did the Secret Service not protect him? Who was the killer?

A man called Lee Harvey Oswald was arrested and accused of murdering a policeman and the president. It was alleged that Oswald had fired from a tall building, the Texas School Book Depository, with a rifle purchased by mail order for only twelve dollars. Two days later, further horror compounded the tragedy as Oswald himself was shot dead by Jack Ruby, in front of millions of television viewers, as he was being moved to a different gaol. These dreadful events had a profound effect on the nation.

The Warren Commission, set up to determine the truth behind the assassination, concluded that Oswald was a communist sympathizer who carried out the assassination on his own. Many people cannot accept this and continue to challenge the Commission's findings. Consider these four questions:

1   Was there a cover up? Was Oswald involved with the FBI or CIA?
2   Was there a conspiracy? Did Castro of Cuba organize the assassination?
3   Is there new evidence? Recent examination of photographs taken of the assassination seems to have revealed a second gunman.
4   Were the mafia involved? Did they have the president murdered because of his war on crime?

These questions are still unanswered, and the majority of Americans believe that the truth will never be known.

Lee Harvey Oswald proclaimed his innocence to reporters before being shot by Jack Ruby.

5
THE USA IN TURMOIL
LBJ and the Great Society

With Jackie Kennedy standing on his left, a grim Lyndon Johnson is sworn in as president immediately after the assassination.

WITH THE DEATH OF President Kennedy, the task of carrying through many of Kennedy's policies fell to Vice-President Lyndon Johnson, known as LBJ. Johnson was in a strong position to do this, in fact he was far more experienced than Kennedy at working with Congress. After the assassination, Johnson warned: 'We have to do something about the hate . . . the roots of hate are poverty and disease and illiteracy, and they are broad in the land.'[43] He launched a 'War on Poverty' which, along with civil rights, formed the cornerstone of what he called the Great Society. The election of 1964 gave Johnson 61.3 per cent of the popular vote. It was not simply an emotional response to the memory of John Kennedy, although that played a part, but an endorsement of Johnson's promise of social reform.

In spite of apparent prosperity, the economy failed to provide jobs with a living wage for at least one fifth of the population. They survived on a family income of less than $3,000 a year. Serious rioting in major cities was a symptom of dreadful deprivation. Johnson persuaded Congress to pass an Economic Opportunity Act to tackle poverty, but his most dramatic success was with the Civil Rights Act of 1964 and the Voting Rights Act of 1965, which finally removed barriers to black Americans being able to vote in the southern states.

Johnson's hopes for a Great Society were constantly thwarted, and were ultimately eclipsed by his greater commitment to defeating the communists in the war in Vietnam. On foreign affairs LBJ was a hawk. 'If the Soviets want America's co-operation,' he said, 'they can earn it. If the Soviets want

America's hostility, they certainly can provide it.'[44] From 1965 onwards, he sent more and more US troops to fight in Vietnam in a war that would prove impossible to win, but that cost thousands of US lives. The war contributed to the anger and protests that were common on the streets. Black American protest spread from the South to the northern cities and became increasingly militant and bitter. A women's movement emerged to challenge their lack of political and economic influence. Disenchanted American Indians campaigned under the banner of Red Power.

Johnson could not understand the strength of opposition to his Vietnam policy. He had pulled the nation together after the death of President Kennedy and he had advocated idealistic policies, but in spite of his Great Society programme unrest and protest were stronger than ever. In 1968 he decided not to seek re-election because of the escalating Vietnam War and the mounting opposition to it.

▶ Johnson's hopes for a Great Society were dragged down by the demands of the Vietnam War. Demonstrations increased as the public turned against the war.

◀ Campaigning for equality under the slogan 'we shall overcome', these black Americans demanded to be served in a restaurant.

Strife in the streets

The 1964 Civil Rights Act to outlaw racial discrimination, and the 1965 Voting Rights Act, were significant advances, and were a major achievement for the non-violent tactics of the black leader, Dr Martin Luther King. However, many young blacks were no longer prepared to put up with the slow progress that came from the patient campaigning that he advocated. Five days after the 1965 Act was signed at the White House, a riot raged through the Watts district of Los Angeles. After a week of violence and looting, 34 people were dead and more than 1,000 injured. The frustration of living in dreadfully run-down city ghettos finally boiled over. Following Watts there were riots in Newark and Detroit, where young rioters burned down their own depressed neighbourhoods.

Between 1964-67, 25 cities suffered serious riots with 142 people killed and 4,700 injured.

Black Power was the uncompromising demand of new young black leaders after 1965. What does the following extract reveal of Dr Martin Luther King's attitude to the riots?

> *I condemn the violence; but I understand the conditions that cause them. I think we must be just as concerned about correcting those conditions as we are about punishing the guilty. I seriously question the will and moral power of this nation to save itself.*[45]

Why did Dr King not condemn those who took part in the riots even though he was

▲ Athletes Tommie Smith and John Carlos defiantly raise their fists in the black power salute at the 1968 Olympic Games.

▲ (Left) Some local laws prohibited mixed-race marriages. It was not until August 1970 that the first inter-racial marriage in Mississippi took place.

opposed to violence? Why do you think he was pessimistic about the ability of the nation to solve the problems?

President Johnson appointed Governor Kerner to head the National Advisory Commission on Civil Disorders to report on the riots. To the unease of many whites the Commission echoed Dr King as it blamed, amongst other things, 'white racism'.

> *What white Americans have never understood is that white society is deeply implicated in the ghetto. White institutions created it, white institutions maintain it, and white society condones it.*
>
> *National action . . . removing the frustrations of powerlessness among the disadvantaged by explicitly helping them to deal with the problems that effect their own lives . . . eliminating all barriers to their choice of jobs, education and housing.*[46]

What did the Commission mean by blaming white Americans for the conditions in the ghettos? How did it suggest the situation could be improved? Why did a white backlash react against the Commission and so make progress more difficult? It was not easy to undo the results of decades of discrimination and economic exploitation. Some improvements were made, but for many black Americans the conditions they lived in remained poor.

The demand for change

Many young people in the 1960s, especially students, adopted radical lifestyles and sometimes radical politics as well. Their behaviour challenged established values, which older people found difficult to tolerate. For example, the hippie counter-culture of drugs, long hair, mystical religions and permissive sexual behaviour, outraged many parents. Hippies questioned a system that tolerated poverty; they campaigned for greater individual freedom, and equality for a range of groups they believed to be oppressed; they opposed the war in Vietnam.

Bob Dylan, a popular 1960s songwriter, expressed in his songs the new creed of protest. What effect would the following lyrics have had on their young audience?

In the 1960's, women's liberation was one of the many protest movements demanding changes in the law and, in this case, in the attitude of men.

come senators congressmen
please heed the call
don't stand in the doorway
don't block up the hall
for he that gets hurt
will be he who has stalled
there's a battle outside raging
it'll soon shake your windows
and rattle your walls
for the times they are changing

come mothers and fathers
throughout the land
and don't criticize
what you can't understand
your sons and daughters
are beyond your command
your old road is rapidly aging
please get out of the new one
if you can't lend your hand
for the times they are changing

From 'The Times They Are Changing'[47]

Violence on a university campus in 1968. People despaired of what was happening in their country.

Why do you think this song became the anthem of the protest movement, and why was it so difficult for parents to understand the rebelliousness of their children? Most of the student campaigners came from comfortable middle-class homes. Their affluence and education gave them the opportunity to rebel.

From 1965 onwards university campuses across the country erupted in protest and violence. Many politicians and older people reacted with fury, accusing students of being ungrateful for the benefits American society gave them. The authorities often used excessive force to end demonstrations, and the students reacted angrily, as this *Newsweek* report describes:

> *To the students, most policemen have become 'pigs', brutal representatives of an uptight power structure.*[48]

Hippies were just one group of a whole range of young questioning individuals. The 1960s were characterized by a mood of protest, a search for meaning in life and alternatives to traditional ways and values. Expressions of frustration and powerlessness broke forth from many people. The women's movement became very active in the 1960s. The manifesto of the National Organization of Women (NOW), set up in 1967, made the following demands:

- Equal rights constitutional amendment.
- Enforcement of laws banning sex discrimination in employment.
- Equal and unsegregated education.
- Equal job training opportunities.

There were many people who derided the women's liberation movement, but the new consciousness of the 1960s enabled women to successfully break down some barriers of sexual discrimination.

The thread of violence

Martin Luther King (second from right) on the balcony of a Memphis hotel; the very place where he was shot dead the following day.

The assassination of President Kennedy and the inner-city riots appalled most Americans. Many people felt a sense of shame that their nation, which prided itself on democratic institutions and a civilized system of justice, should breed such violence.

On 4 April 1968, the most important leader of black Americans, Dr Martin Luther King, was shot dead in Memphis, Tennessee. He had constantly preached non-violence, but his death prompted massive rioting among black people angry and in despair over his death. Two months later Senator Robert Kennedy, brother of President Kennedy, was also murdered as he campaigned for the presidency. The nightmare of Dallas had been repeated, as once again violence intervened in the political process. In fact, not only political assassination and murder, but all crimes of violence were increasing in the USA. What does the graph below tell you about the incidence of

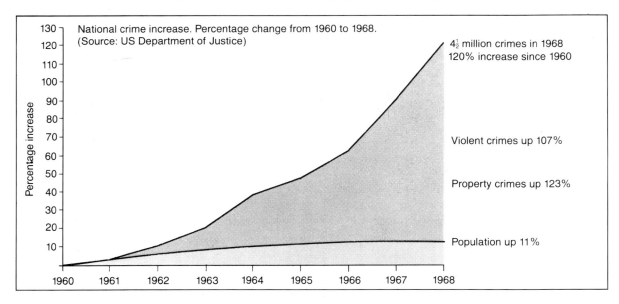

National crime increase. Percentage change from 1960 to 1968.
(Source: US Department of Justice)

$4\frac{1}{2}$ million crimes in 1968
120% increase since 1960

Violent crimes up 107%

Property crimes up 123%

Population up 11%

People were appalled when Senator Robert Kennedy became another victim of political assassination in June 1968.

crime between 1960–68? Bear in mind the fact that reported crime rises do not necessarily mean an increase in crime, but merely in the number of offences reported.

Americans were horrified at the spiral of violence in the country and the apparent powerlessness of the government to stop it. In spite of the USA's great wealth and the military strength of a superpower, it was the threat of crime that frightened people the most. How did the assassination of leaders fit into the general pattern of violence?

With more than fifty million guns in private hands there was a strong case for tough gun control. The second amendment of the American Constitution guarantees that, 'The right of the people to bear arms shall not be infringed'; but in 1791 when that amendment was agreed there was a clear need for armed civilians ready to defend the security of the country. In the 1960s, the powerful gun lobby used this

clause to support their argument that all citizens should be allowed a gun. Following the death of Robert Kennedy, President Johnson appealed for new gun control laws:

> *On many occasions before, I have spoken of the terrible toll inflicted on our people by firearms – 750,000 Americans dead since the turn of the century . . . Weapons of destruction can be purchased by mail as easily as baskets of fruit or cartons of cigarettes. We must eliminate the dangers of mail-order murder in this country.* [49]

The president's fervent attempt to restrict gun sales was thwarted by the gun lobby. Why do you think it proved impossible to limit the sale and ownership of guns? It is surprising that after an unsettled period of violence and assassinations the Congress was unwilling to pass effective gun legislation. It remained easy not only to buy hunting rifles but also the handguns known as 'Saturday night specials'.

Vietnam: hawks and doves

By early 1968, the conflict in Vietnam had become the longest and most unpopular foreign war in the USA's history. It divided the nation and badly scarred its pride. In the early 1960s, President Kennedy had sent advisers to assist South Vietnam in defeating guerrillas supported by communist North Vietnam. President Johnson increased American military presence until there were over 400,000 US combat troops in Vietnam. At home the hawks (as those who supported the US action were known) advocated a military victory, with some even suggesting the use of nuclear weapons. The doves (those who opposed intervention in Vietnam) campaigned for the withdrawal of American forces.

The question why Johnson sent so many troops to fight in Vietnam has no easy answer. Compare the following two sources. The first is a Secret Defense Department memorandum, dated 24 March 1965; the second is from a speech President Johnson made on 7 April 1965.

United States aims in Vietnam

70%	To avoid a humiliating US defeat.
20%	To keep South Vietnam territory from Chinese hands.
10%	To permit the people of South Vietnam to enjoy a better, freer way of life.[50]

Our objective is the independence of South Vietnam, and its freedom from attack. We want nothing for ourselves – only that the people of South Vietnam be allowed to guide their own country in their own way.[51]

◄ Scenes like this, shown on television, persuaded many to oppose the war.

▼ An anti-Vietnam War poster, parodying the First World War Uncle Sam recruitment posters.

Consider the dates of the two sources, and their intended audiences. Can you see a contradiction between the Defense Department memorandum and the president's speech? Why do you think this was?

In the summer of 1968, public opposition to the war was very strong. What explanation for this feeling can you draw from the following statistics?

American troops in Vietnam[52]

Nov. 1963	16,500
Nov. 1964	25,000
Dec. 1965	180,000
Dec. 1966	380,000
Dec. 1967	450,000

American deaths in Vietnam[53]

1965	1,728
1966	6,053
1967	11,048
(Jan–June) 1968	10,503

Television brought the horror of the fighting into everyone's home. North Vietnam's leader, Ho Chi Minh, criticized the USA's intervention:

Vietnam is thousands of miles away from the United States. The Vietnamese people have never done any harm to the United States . . . The US Government has ceaselessly intervened in Vietnam; it has unleashed and intensified the war of aggression.[54]

The Americans dropped more bombs on Vietnam than on enemy territory in the Second World War, yet they could not defeat the communists. Robert Kennedy pronounced against the USA's involvement:

Do we have a right here in the United States, to say that we're going to kill tens of thousands, make millions of people homeless, kill women and children? I very seriously question whether we have that right.[55]

The pressure to end the war was enormous. But it was difficult for the USA to pull out without considerable humiliation.

Vietnam in the 1960s. The North Vietnam communist government kept the rebel Viet Cong in the south supplied with weapons via the Ho Chi Minh trail.

6
DETENTE AND WATERGATE
President Nixon

ONSERVATISM TRIUMPHED IN 1968 with the election of Richard Nixon. The middle class and much of the blue collar or working class rallied to Nixon's reassertion of traditional values, including law and order and a belief in the American dream of personal success. His election was a reaction against the protests, the civil rights campaigns and supposed moral permissiveness, as the 'silent majority' of Americans (as Nixon called his supporters) voted for a Republican. He was a tough politician who had made his name through strong speeches during the cold war of the early 1950s. His vice-president, Spiro Agnew, was even more conservative and blamed the 'pointy heads', as he called intellectuals, for the protests and demonstrations.

The major concern in 1968 was the Vietnam War. Nixon promised to bring the war to an honourable conclusion, but it dragged on, and in fact in 1970 Nixon extended the conflict into neighbouring Cambodia. This provoked even greater anti-war protests within the USA, including one at Kent State University when four students were shot dead by the Ohio National Guard. Nixon soon had to abandon the slogan 'Bring Us Together' which he had used at the start of his presidency.

Nixon's achievements have been overshadowed by the scandal which ended his presidency. In 1972 he surprised the world

Nixon and Agnew were elected to stop the violence at home and to end the war.

One of the students killed at Kent State University during an anti-war demonstration in 1970.

by becoming the first US president to visit China, and he did eventually begin to pull US forces out of Vietnam in 1973. Ironically Nixon's career had been built on tough anti-communism, yet his visit to China and then to Moscow three months later were diplomatic triumphs that began a new period of East-West détente.

At the end of 1971, *Time* magazine declared him its Man of the Year, 'He made his bid for a historic niche on the issues of war and peace . . . the standards he has set for his tenure are high.'[56] In 1972, Nixon and Agnew were re-elected by a landslide. It seemed that his old nickname from the early 1960s, Tricky Dick, was forgotten and even his critics spoke of a 'new Nixon'. However, during 1973 and 1974, scandalous

revelations of political dishonesty surfaced which totally destroyed Nixon's credibility. The Watergate affair, as it became known, shocked the nation, and it was a great relief when he finally resigned. Nixon's embarrassment was compounded by Vice-President Agnew resigning over unrelated allegations of corruption. They are the only people ever to resign from those high positions. It is ironic that the president who put great store by law and order, resigned to avoid possible impeachment. Nixon probably only avoided prosecution because of the pardon given him by his successor, President Ford.

Peace and détente

Richard Nixon surprised people by going to communist China, but his visit in 1972 was a great diplomatic success.

The Vietnam War created deep divisions and anguish in the USA as it became clear that the US Army was involved in a terrible war that it could not win. The North Vietnamese demand was straightforward – total US withdrawal from Vietnam. President Nixon blamed North Vietnam for refusing to negotiate, but could Nixon's address to the nation in May 1969 be described as conciliatory?

The enemy is counting on a collapse of American will in the United States . . . our fighting men are not going to be worn down; our mediators are not going to be talked down.[57]

In the end the USA was desperate to disentangle itself from the Vietnam War at any price, and in January 1973, Nixon spoke on television in quite a different tone:

Good evening. I have asked for this radio and television time tonight for the purpose of announcing that we today have concluded an agreement to end the war and bring peace with honor in Vietnam and South-East Asia.[58]

It is easy to understand the sense of relief, but was there really any honour? The complete failure of the USA's Vietnam policy became clear in April 1975 when the communist North Vietnamese took over the whole country.

Considering US policy in Vietnam, Nixon's diplomatic initiatives towards détente with China and the USSR represented a sharp and surprising shift away from the former hostility. Nixon was the first US president to visit these communist countries. The secretary of state, Henry Kissinger, made a clear explanatory statement in the case of China:

> *We are pursuing our policy . . . on the ground that a stable peace . . . is difficult to envisage if 800 million people are excluded from a dialogue with the most powerful nation in the world.*[59]

Does this extract reveal a practical, or an idealistic policy? Do you think it was arrogant, or realistic to refer to the USA as 'the most powerful nation in the world.'? What effect was the USA's experience in Vietnam likely to have had in deciding this new policy? Americans were surprised but agreeable to their president visiting China.

Panic surrounded the retreat of the last US diplomats from South Vietnam as the communists took over in 1975.

Harris opinion poll[60]

Do you approve or disapprove of President Nixon visiting China?

Approve	68%
Disapprove	19%
No opinion	13%

Three months after his visit to China, Nixon went to Moscow. Obviously the suspicion and distrust of several decades could not be wiped out by a single visit, but thinking back to events since 1945, why were these visits considered so encouraging? One result was a step forward in beginning to limit the numbers of nuclear weapons with which each side threatened the other, through agreements known as SALT (Strategic Arms Limitation Treaty). The USA was not abandoning its policy of stopping the spread of communism but it did now accept the need for peaceful coexistence with the two great communist powers.

Watergate

Nixon, with his wife and daughter, at the time of his resignation. The public were horrified by the stream of revelations about the president's behaviour over the Watergate affair.

The Watergate scandal destroyed Richard Nixon and undermined the presidency itself. During the 1972 election campaign, five men were caught red-handed attempting to burgle the Democratic National Committee office in the Watergate building in Washington DC. At least one burglar had direct links with the Republican campaign to re-elect Nixon. Although the president denied any advance knowledge of the burglary, he nevertheless conducted a massive cover-up involving close White House colleagues. Investigators and journalists doggedly pursued the truth. Nixon was even prepared to buy people's silence, and

in a manner more of a mafia leader than of a president, he asked his special adviser John Dean:

> Nixon: 'How much do you need?'
> Dean: 'I would say these people are going to cost a million dollars over the next two years.'
> Nixon: 'We could get that. On the money, if you need the money you could get that. You could get it in cash. I know where it could be gotten.'[61]

In 1974, when Congress forced Nixon to release transcripts of his private conversations that he had secretly taped, Americans were horrified to learn of the president's behaviour.

Widespread disbelief met Nixon's increasingly implausible explanations for his actions. What does this survey indicate of public confidence?

Do you believe those who run the government
are crooked?
Yes 53%
Do you want the president removed from office?
Yes 49%
No 14%
Undecided 37%[62]

Why did people turn so vehemently against Richard Nixon? The enormous pressure on him was increased still more when Congress voted by 410 votes to only 4 against to consider his impeachment. Nixon's humiliation was finally completed on 8 August 1974 when he told a somewhat relieved nation that he was at last resigning:

Nixon had no choice but to resign over Watergate. American confidence was severely shaken by the scandal.

I have never been a quitter. To leave office before my term is completed is abhorrent to every instinct in my body. But as president, I must put the interest of America first.[63]

Louis Heren, a British journalist, wrote that, 'the modern American president has assumed powers similar to those of an English monarch . . . Nixon acted as did some of those old kings.'[64] Critics of the USA were quick to seize on Watergate as evidence of a corrupt political system, but others argued that the resignation of the president, as a result of the perseverance of reporters and Congressional investigators, vindicated the American system of government. However, the public's view that politicians could not be trusted was strengthened and Watergate altered the way that Americans regarded their leaders.

7

REDEFINING THE USA'S ROLE
Ford and Carter

NIXON'S SUCCESSORS, FORD and Carter, sought to restore the confidence of people in their government and to redefine the USA's role in the world. On taking office after Watergate Gerald Ford told Americans, that:

> *Our long national nightmare is over. Our Constitution works. Our great Republic is a government of laws and not of men.*[65]

Why did President Ford emphasise the role of the Constitution and the law in the government? In 1976, the memory of Watergate helped Democrat Jimmy Carter to decisively defeat President Ford. Almost immediately, however, the new president was tainted by scandal when his close friend, Bert Lance, was forced to resign from a senior government post after allegations of financial improprieties.

President Carter was determined that the USA would be involved in tackling major world problems, and would not leave any vacuum that the USSR could fill. In 1975, the Helsinki Agreement had promised closer East-West co-operation and greater freedom for Soviet citizens. Carter criticized the USSR over its human rights record, and after the Soviet invasion of Afghanistan he initiated the US boycott of the 1980 Moscow Olympics. Many nations considered this a controversial act, and critics accused the USA of hypocrisy over human rights, pointing out its support for the unpopular Shah of Iran and the dictatorships in Chile and the Philippines.

Carter's major diplomatic success was in securing an agreement between the two old Middle East adversaries, Israel and Egypt.

Gerald Ford had the difficult task of restoring people's confidence in their leaders after Watergate, but damaged his own standing by granting a full pardon to Nixon.

In 1979 the president managed to bring the leaders of the two nations together to sign a peace treaty at the presidential retreat, Camp David. It was the high point of the Carter presidency.

In 1979 a revolution in Iran deposed the Shah, a staunch ally of the USA, and

President Carter permitted him to enter the USA. The new Iranian Government was strongly anti-American, and in November of that year thousands of Iranians seized the US Embassy and held sixty-five Americans hostage. It is easy to understand the anger and frustration of the president and public. The USA appeared powerless and an attempted rescue mission was a tragic fiasco with eight Americans killed. Carter's reputation declined, and in the election of 1980 he was heavily defeated by Republican Ronald Reagan. On election day, Jimmy Carter wrote in his diary:

Most of the things we did that were difficult and controversial cost us votes in the long run. Camp David accords, opening up Africa, dealing with the Cuban refugees, Panama Canal treaties, the normalization with China, energy legislation, plus the hostages and the Soviet invasion of Afghanistan – particularly the hostages.[66]

Was President Carter entitled to feel a little bitter?

On the day that Jimmy Carter handed over to Ronald Reagan, the hostages, after 444 days in captivity in Iran, were released.

In 1979 Carter brought Begin of Israel and Sadat of Egypt to Camp David to sign the historic Camp David Treaty. This was perhaps the crowning success of Carter's presidency.

The Reagan years

Ronald Reagan was a popular president with strong conservative views. He advocated a tough stand against any perceived spread of communism in the western hemisphere. Billions of dollars were given to the pro-American Contra rebels, for example, that were fighting to overthrow the left wing Sandanista government that ruled the 2.8 million people of Nicaragua. There were understandable worries that the USA might be drawn into a Vietnam-style war in Nicaragua, and Congress prevented any military involvement and restricted further aid to the Contras.

Reagan also asserted the USA's right to interfere in other countries when US Marines invaded the British Commonwealth island of Grenada to prevent a left wing government from taking control. Although the United Nations condemned the military action, it was widely applauded by American public opinion. Why do you think Americans approved of President Reagan's action?

When Reagan became president in 1981 he was strongly antagonistic towards the communist East, in 1983 publicly referring to the USSR as an 'evil empire'. However, during the 1980s with a new era of *glasnost* in the USSR, Reagan and the Soviet leader, Gorbachev, met in a series of sometimes difficult summit meetings. From these summits resulted some momentous agreements, that once seemed quite impossible, to reduce the nuclear weapons of both powers.

A serious scandal during his second term threatened to damage Reagan's reputation. Senior officials, including Colonel Oliver North, illegally arranged to supply arms to Iran and use the cash raised to help the Contra rebels in Nicaragua. The Iran-Contra scandal led to the resignations of senior White House staff, and Colonel North faced

President Reagan, seconds before an assassination attempt on 30 March 1981. Reagan made a complete recovery.

Colonel Oliver North, giving evidence to Congress in 1987. The Iran-Contra scandal threatened to ruin President Reagan's reputation.

serious charges. Investigations failed to link the president directly to the scandal but it cast doubts on his authority over his staff.

In October 1987 the stock market crashed disastrously. President Reagan was blamed for the poor state of the economy and the serious budget deficit caused by government overspending. At the same time there were worries and demands for action on problems of pollution and the environment, race and discrimination, drugs and crime. Despite these problems, Ronald Reagan remained a popular, if not entirely successful, president.

Reagan's vice-president George Bush was elected president in 1988 by a clear majority, but the same election returned a strongly Democratic Congress. In many ways the USA remains a deeply divided nation. One question for the future is that posed by Alistair Cooke, the broadcaster:

What is the quality and staying power of American civilization? Every other country scorns American materialism, while striving in every big and little way to match it. Envy obviously has something to do with it, but there is a true basis for this debate, it is whether America is in its ascendant or its decline.[67]

Leading figures

James E. Carter (1924–)

Jimmy Carter, a peanut farmer from the Deep South, surprised many people by emerging from the relative obscurity of Georgia state politics to win the 1976 presidential election on behalf of the Democratic Party. A deeply religious man, he took a strong line against what he saw as the denial of human rights in the USSR, and proposed the American boycott of the 1980 Moscow Olympic Games. He successfully arranged peace talks leading to agreement between Israel and her old enemy, Egypt. But he was less successful in dealing with the new Iranian government of Ayatollah Khomeini. His failure to secure the release of American officials held hostage in Iran badly damaged his reputation. Within his own party he was challenged by Senator Edward Kennedy. In 1980 Carter failed to be re-elected and returned home to Plains, Georgia.

Fidel Castro (1927–)

Fidel Castro organized and led the Cuban revolution that overthrew the repressive and dictatorial Batista regime in 1959. As leader of Cuba, Castro angered the USA by taking over American-owned land and businesses. The USA stopped trade with Cuba and broke off diplomatic relations as Castro turned increasingly to the USSR for military and economic support. His decision to permit Soviet missiles to be based in Cuba led to the 1962 missile crisis. Castro's government survived these problems but to many Americans he has remained a figure of intense and probably unjustified hatred and fear.

Dwight D. Eisenhower (1890–1969)

Dwight Eisenhower graduated in 1915 from the West Point military academy and rose rapidly through the ranks in the US Army. During the Second World War he commanded American forces in Europe and his success in commanding the allied forces in the 1944 D-Day invasion made him a

Jimmy Carter served only one term as president.

national hero. After the war he was approached by both the Republicans and Democrats to enter politics. In 1952 he accepted the Republican nomination and led the party to a comfortable victory over his liberal Democrat opponent, Adlai Stevenson. Eisenhower saw himself as a political moderate and was held in great popular affection. He provided the nation with stability, although some critics accuse him of ignoring the problems that were to cause difficulties in the 1960s.

Gerald R. Ford (1913–)

Gerald Ford was never elected to the presidency. He had served for twenty-five years as a Republican in the House of Representatives when President Nixon appointed him vice-president to replace Vice-President Agnew who had resigned. When Nixon resigned in 1974, Ford moved into the White House. He tried hard to restore faith in the presidency after the Watergate scandals, but damaged his own standing by granting a full pardon to Nixon. He had an unfortunate reputation for clumsiness, and unkind jokes questioned his ability to be president. He failed to be elected in 1976.

Lyndon B. Johnson (1908–1973)

Lyndon Johnson, a Texan, entered the House of Representatives in 1937 and was elected to the Senate in 1948. By 1953 he was Democratic leader in the Senate, and in 1960 was a top contender for the Democratic presidential nomination. Beaten in that by John Kennedy, he did accept with some reluctance the nomination for vice-president. He played a key part in Kennedy's narrow victory by winning the support of southern voters. Following the assassination of President Kennedy, Johnson succeeded to the presidency and was elected in his own right in 1964. Responsible for many important reforms, he aroused strong opposition over his Vietnam policy. Seriously challenged within his own party, he decided not to seek re-election in 1968 and retired to his Texas ranch.

John F. Kennedy (1917–1963)

At the age of forty-three, Kennedy was the youngest-ever elected president and the first Roman Catholic to occupy the office. After studying at the London School of Economics in Britain, and Harvard University in the USA, he served in the Second World War as commander of a PT boat. He became a hero when he saved members of his crew after they had been sunk by a Japanese destroyer. He entered the House of Representatives in 1946 and went on to enter the Senate in 1952. By 1960 he and his wife, Jacqueline, were popular national figures. In a tough electoral contest, Kennedy defeated his Republican rival, Richard Nixon, by a very slim majority to become president in 1961. His popularity and stature grew in the White House so that his assassination appalled the nation and the world. He is buried at Arlington National Cemetery in Washington DC.

Eisenhower lacked strong political views, but he succeeded in winning two elections, and he remained popular throughout his terms of office.

Robert F. Kennedy (1925–1968)

Robert Kennedy was the younger brother of President Kennedy and played a great part in organizing his political campaigns. He became attorney-general, the nation's top legal official, in his brother's Cabinet. Following the assassination of John Kennedy, Robert assumed the leadership of the large Kennedy family. Many of those who had supported President Kennedy looked to Robert to continue the work of his brother, and he was elected to the Senate in 1964. He was critical of the Vietnam War, and in 1968 decided to run for the presidency. He was a symbol of hope to many, but his campaign came to a tragic end when he, too, was assassinated. Robert Kennedy now lies buried next to the grave of his brother John.

Dr Martin Luther King (1929–1968)

As a young black clergyman from the southern state of Georgia, Dr King emerged as an articulate and brave champion of racial justice. He preached non-violent resistance, and organized mass demonstrations and protests against segregation. In 1963 he led 200,000 people on the march on Washington

◀ Martin Luther King was the USA's most important civil rights leader. He organized mass demonstrations but always opposed violence, and in 1964 he was awarded the Nobel Peace Prize. His murder prompted widespread rioting.

▶ President Harry S. Truman.

54

at which he made his most famous speech: 'I have a dream that one day this nation will rise up and live out the true meaning of its creed: we hold these truths to be self-evident, that all men are created equal.' His impressive leadership helped to dismantle segregation. But racial prejudice remained, and Dr King became a focus for white extremists' hatred. In 1968, whilst supporting a strike by Memphis refuse workers, he was shot and killed.

Richard M. Nixon (1913–)

Richard Nixon, a Republican, has to endure the shame of being the only president to have resigned from office. He was elected to the House of Representatives in 1946 and soon achieved prominence by making strong attacks on communism at home and abroad. He was not always a particularly popular person and was often accused by his opponents of being untrustworthy; the nickname 'Tricky Dick' remained with him. He served briefly in the Senate before being chosen as vice-president under Eisenhower. In spite of his eight years in that position he was defeated by Kennedy when he ran for president in 1960. However, eight years later, partly as a reaction to the turmoil of the 1960s, the voters turned to Nixon. He was the first president to visit China and

the USSR and he finally ended American involvement in Vietnam. The Watergate scandals revealed serious personal misconduct and behaviour unfitting for a president. He resigned in disgrace in August 1974.

Ronald W. Reagan (1911–)

At the age of sixty-nine, Ronald Reagan was the oldest man to be elected president. A Hollywood movie and television actor, he became involved in Republican politics and was elected Governor of California in 1964. He took a stern line against student protests and defended tough action by the police. He soon became the leading spokesman of the conservative wing of the Republican Party and a vigorous defender of traditional American values. This appealed to many voters and he became president in 1980. His personality rather than his achievements helped him win re-election in 1984. In spite of some doubts about his negotiating skills his second term was marked by warmer relations with the USSR.

Harry S. Truman (1884–1972)

Harry Truman grew up in Independence, Missouri. After serving in the First World War, he set up a men's clothing store which went bankrupt in 1921. During the 1920s he studied law and became active in the Democratic Party. In 1934 he was elected to the Senate as a strong supporter of Roosevelt's New Deal programme. Ten years later the Democrats selected him to serve as vice-president, and with Roosevelt's sudden death in 1945 he became president. Some doubted his abilities and criticized his blunt manner and strong language, but he proved popular and was elected in his own right in 1948. Truman had to deal with difficult post-war problems and took a tough line on communism. He lost public support over the failure to secure the total defeat of North Korea in the Korean War and this was one important reason why he declined to stand again in 1952 and instead retired to Independence, Missouri.

Important dates

<table>
<tr><td colspan="2" align="center">Events</td><td></td></tr>
<tr><td>Date</td><td>USA</td><td>Rest of the World</td></tr>
</table>

Date	USA	Date	Rest of the World
1945	President Roosevelt dies. Vice-President Truman (Democrat) becomes 33rd president. First atomic bomb is dropped on Japan.	1945	Second World War ends. United Nations set up.
1948	Truman re-elected president. The Marshall Plan.	1948	USSR blockades Berlin. Berlin airlift.
1949	NATO set up.		
1950–53	Korean War.		
1952	Eisenhower (Republican) elected 34th president, with Richard Nixon as vice-president. First H-bomb test.	1953	Death of the Soviet leader, Stalin. First Soviet H-bomb test.
1954	Televised Senator McCarthy – US Army hearings. Supreme Court rules racial segregation in schools is unconstitutional.	1954	Khrushchev becomes leader of the USSR.
1955	Dr Martin Luther King begins career as civil rights leader.	1955	Warsaw Pact created.
1956	Eisenhower re-elected.	1956	Polish and Hungarian uprisings crushed. Suez crisis.
1957	Violence at Little Rock High School over desegregation.	1957	USSR launches Sputnik satellite. Civil war begins in Vietnam.
1958	First US satellite to go into orbit, Explorer 1.		
1959	Soviet leader Khrushchev visits the USA.	1959	Cuban Revolution led by Fidel Castro.
1960	John Kennedy (Democrat) elected 35th president, with Lyndon Johnson as vice-president.		
1961	Bay of Pigs invasion of Cuba was repulsed.	1961	Berlin Wall built. USSR puts first man into space.
1962	First American in space. Cuban missile crisis.		
1963	President Kennedy assassinated. Vice-President Johnson becomes 36th president.	1963	Partial Nuclear Test Ban Treaty.
1964	Civil Rights Act.	1964	Khrushchev deposed in the USSR.
1965	Voting Rights Act guarantees voting rights for all citizens. Combat troops sent to Vietnam. Rise of black protest movements.		
		1967	Arab-Israeli Six-Day War.
1968	Dr Martin Luther King assassinated. Rise of anti-war protest movement. Senator Robert Kennedy assassinated. Richard Nixon (Republican) elected 37th president, with Spiro Agnew as vice-president.	1968	Violent student riots in Paris. Strong anti-Vietnam War protests in Britain. USSR invades Czechoslovakia.

Date	USA		Rest of the World
1969	Woodstock rock festival. American astronauts become first men on the moon.		
1970	US troops invade Cambodia. Four students shot dead in anti-war protest at Kent State University. Strategic arms agreement with the USSR.		
1972	Nixon and Agnew re-elected. Watergate burglary. SALT-I Treaty. *February* Nixon visited China. *May* Nixon visited USSR.		
1973	USA begins withdrawal from Vietnam. Vice-President Agnew resigns. Gerald Ford appointed vice-president.	1973	Elected government in Chile replaced by military dictatorship. Arab-Israeli Yom Kippur War. Oil crisis.
1974	Nixon resigns. Ford (Republican) becomes 38th president.		
		1975	Communists take over the whole of Vietnam.
1976	USA celebrates its Bicentennial. Jimmy Carter (Democrat) elected 39th president, with Walter Mondale as vice-president.		
1979	President Carter arranges Camp David peace agreement between Israel and Egypt. US Embassy staff in Iran held hostage (for 444 days). Carter signs the SALT-II Treaty, but the US Senate refuse to ratify it.	1979	Sandanista government takes power in Nicaragua. Iranian Revolution, Shah of Iran ousted. USSR invades Afghanistan.
1980	USA boycotts Moscow Olympic Games. Ronald Reagan (Republican) elected 40th president, with George Bush as vice-president.	1980	Start of the Iran-Iraq War.
1981	Assassination attempt wounds President Reagan.		
1982	Equal Rights Amendment (ERA) to the Constitution fails to be ratified by sufficient number of states.	1982	Israel invades Lebanon. USSR rules out first use of nuclear weapons. Falklands War.
1983	Star Wars idea begins.		
1984	Reagan and Bush re-elected.		
1985	Reagan and Gorbachev meet in Geneva.	1985	Gorbachev becomes leader of the USSR.
1986	US planes bomb Libya. Summit meeting at Reykjavik.		
1987	Gorbachev visits USA and signs the INF Treaty.		
1988	Reagan visits Moscow and London. George Bush (Republican) elected 41st president, with Dan Quayle as vice-president.	1988	USSR begins withdrawal from Afghanistan. Gorbachev announces unilateral cuts in Soviet troops. End of the Iran-Iraq War.

Glossary

Affluent	Possessing wealth.
Amendment	An alteration to a law or resolution. A Constitutional amendment alters or adds to the Constitution.
Armistice	Agreement to stop fighting.
Assassination	The murder of an important politician or official.
Brinkmanship	Pressing a dangerous situation to the limit, or brink, of safety and peace.
Cabinet	The president's committee of the heads of the major government departments.
Camelot	Name given to the legendary court of King Arthur, and after 1960 applied to President Kennedy's White House.
Camp David	Country retreat used by presidents.
Capitalist	A believer in the virtue of free enterprise, and the right to individual property and wealth.
CIA	Central Intelligence Agency responsible for collecting intelligence information on possible enemies.
Civil rights	Rights and liberties of citizens. The phrase is often used to refer to the rights of black Americans.
Communism	A political and economic theory following the ideas of Karl Marx who believed in the abolition of all private property and the creation of a classless society.
Conciliatory	To be friendly and prepared to compromise.
Confederacy	Eleven southern states that went to war against the northern states in the Civil War, 1861–65.
Congress	The legislative or law-making branch of the government. It comprises the House of Representatives and the Senate.
Conservative	Favouring the preservation of established customs and values. Someone opposed to excessive or rapid change.
Constitution	The rules and principles by which the government is organized.
Democracy	Rule by the people or their elected representatives.
Desegregation	To get rid of segregation (q.v.).
Détente	Friendlier relations between nations. A relaxing of tension.
Dissent	Disagreement and protest.
Electoral college	Persons who cast the electoral vote of each state for president and vice-president. Each state has electoral votes equal to its total number of Representatives and Senators in Congress. The votes are cast on the basis of who wins the popular vote in the state.
Equal rights amendment	Proposal to include in the Constitution a prohibition of sex discrimination. It failed to be agreed by the necessary three-quarters of the states and so was defeated.
FBI	Federal Bureau of Investigation, responsible for investigating violations of federal law.
Federal government	The central or national government based in Washington DC.
Ghetto	Poor city neighbourhood inhabited by one racial group.
Glasnost	The new policy of open discussion in the USSR started by Gorbachev.
Guerrilla	Member of an irregular force, usually politically motivated, fighting an organized, regular army.
Hobo	A tramp or migrant worker.
Hippie	Person rejecting conventional standards of dress and behaviour and

	choosing greater freedom in morals and conduct. Hippies are often associated with drugs and 1960s rock music.
Impeachment	Accusation of a crime against the president or other high official.
Inaugural address	Speech made at the Inauguration, the formal ceremony when the new president takes office.
Interdict	To prohibit.
Isolationists	People who believe the USA should avoid any political or military involvements with other countries.
Left wing	Left wing ideas advocate change and oppose conservatism. Left-wingers usually support some form of socialism.
Legislature	Branch of government that makes the laws: US Congress.
Liberal	Someone with social and political views favouring reform and individual freedom.
Mafia	A secret international criminal organization.
NASA	National Aeronautics and Space Administration.
National Guard	Soldiers under the command of the governor in each state.
Prohibition	The outlawing of alcoholic drinks from 1919–1933.
Racial discrimination	Treating someone differently, usually badly, because of their race.
Radical	Someone who seeks great change in society, usually associated with left wing politics.
Secretary of state	Government official responsible for foreign affairs.
Segregation	Keeping races separate from each other, usually to the detriment of black Americans in the southern states.
Stars and Stripes	Flag of the USA.
State department	Government department responsible for foreign affairs.
Subversion	Efforts to undermine the government.
USSR	Union of Soviet Socialist Republics.
Vice-president	A deputy to the president, elected on the same ticket as the president. The vice-president takes over if the president dies or is removed from office.
Washington DC	The capital of the USA and centre of government located in the District of Columbia.
White House	The residence and office of the president.
Witch-hunt	Unfair accusations against political opponents.

Further reading

Text Books
Bailey, T., and Kennedy, D., *The American Pageant*, D.C. Heath, Lexington, 1979.
Brogan, H., *Longman History of the United States of America*, Longman, 1985.
Brogan, H., *Pelican History of the United States of America*, Penguin, 1986.
Denenburg, R.V., *Understanding American Politics*, Fontana, 1976.
Estall, R., *A Modern Geography of the United States*, Penguin, 1976.
Issell, W., *Social Change in the United States 1945–1983*, Macmillan, 1985.
O'Callaghan, D.B., *The United States Since 1945*, Longman, 1983.
Shannon, D., *Twentieth Century America*, Rand McNally, Chicago, 1969.

Easier Books
Cooke, A., *America*, BBC Books, 1973.
Baker, P., *Martin Luther King*, Wayland, 1974.
Brown, P., and Schloredt, V., *Martin Luther King*, Exley, 1988.
Harris, J., *The Long Freedom Road*, Constable Young Books, 1968.
Heren, L., *The Story of America*, Times Books, 1976.
Leapman, M., *The US Election*, Coronet, 1988.
Manchester, W., *One Brief Shining Moment: Remembering Kennedy*, Michael Joseph, 1983.
Wolfe, T., *The Right Stuff*, Bantam, 1981.
Williams, J., *Eyes on the Prize*, Harrap, 1987.

Scholarly Books
Carroll, P.N., and Noble, D.W., *The Free and the Unfree*, Penguin, 1977.
Diggins, J.P., *The Proud Decades*, Norton, New York, 1988.
Halberstam, *The Best and Brightest*, New York, 1972.
Piers, B., *Ike: The Life and Times of Dwight D. Eisenhower*, Secker & Warburg, 1987.
Schlesinger, A., *Robert Kennedy and his Times*, André Deutsch, 1978.
Sorensen, T., *Kennedy*, Hodder and Stoughton, 1965.

Original Sources
Bernstein, C., and Woodward, B., *All the President's Men*, Secker & Warburg, 1974.
Bernstein, C., and Woodward, B., *The Final Days*, Secker & Warburg, 1976.
Carter, J., *Keeping Faith*, Collins, 1982.
Ford, G., *A Time to Heal*, W.H. Allen, 1979.
Johnson, L.B., *The Vantage Point*, Weidenfeld & Nicolson, 1972.
Nixon, R., *Six Crises*, Doubleday, New York, 1962.
Truman, H., *The Truman Memoirs* Vol. 1 & 2, Hodder and Stoughton, 1955.
White, T.H., *The Making of the President*, Jonathan Cape, 1965.

Acknowledgements

The author and publishers would like to thank Bob Dylan for permission to use the lyrics from 'The Times They Are Changing' (p36); and the following for allowing their illustrations to be used in this book: Camera Press 22, 31 (Robert Jackson/Dallas Time Herald), 39 (Lawrence Schiller), 42, 44, 48, 49, (Karl Schumacher), 52 (Diana Walker), 54; John Frost 8, 12, 19; Peter Newark's Western Americana 4, 5 (both), 9 (top), 20, 23, 27, 30, 32, 38, 40 (bottom); Photri 7, 9 (bottom), 14 (both), 16, 21, 26; Popperfoto 10, 11, 13, 17, 18, 24, 28, 29, 33 (top), 34, 35 (right), 36, 37, 40 (top), 43, 45, 46, 47, 50, 51; The Research House cover; Topham 6, 53, 55; Wayland Picture Library 15, 33 (bottom), 35 (left). The maps on pages 13, 19, 25, 29 and 41 were supplied by Thames Cartographic Services Ltd., the graph on page 38 was supplied by Malcolm Walker.

Notes on sources

1 Cited in Carroll, P.N., & Noble, D.W., *The Free and the Unfree*, Penguin, 1977.
2 *Ibid.*
3 Cited in MacGregor Burns, J., *Roosevelt – The Soldier of Freedom*, Harcourt Brace Jovanovich, New York, 1970.
4 Cited in Truman, M., *Harry S. Truman*, Morrow, New York, 1972.
5 Kennan, G., 'The Sources of Soviet Conduct', *Foreign Affairs*, 25 July 1947, USA.
6 Furer, H. (ed.), *Harry Truman Presidential Documents*, Oceana, New York, 1970.
7 Cited in Acheson, D., *Present at the Creation*, Norton, New York, 1969.
8 Cited in Time Life, *This Incredible Century: The Fifties*, Time Life Books, New York, 1970.
9 Furer, *op.cit.*
10 Truman, *op.cit.*
11 *Gallup Opinion Polls*, New York, 1951.
12 *Ibid.*
13 Cited in Shannon, D., *Twentieth Century America*, Rand McNally, Chicago, 1969.
14 Cited in Bailey, T., and Kennedy, D., *The American Pageant*, D.C. Heath, Lexington, 1979.
15 Time Life *op.cit.*
16 Bailey, E., *Joe McCarthy and the Press*, University of Wisconsin, Wisconsin, 1981.
17 *Ibid.*
18 *Ibid.*
19 *Gallup Opinion Polls*, New York, 1957.
20 Shannon, *op.cit.*
21 Vexler, R. (ed.), *Dwight Eisenhower: Presidential Documents*, Oceana, New York, 1970.
22 *Ibid.*
23 Time Life, *op.cit.*
24 Shannon, *op.cit.*
25 Galbraith, J.K., *The Affluent Society*, Signet, New York, 1958.
26 Harrington, M., *The Other America*, Penguin, New York, 1963.
27 Sorensen, T., *Kennedy*, Hodder and Stoughton, London, 1965.
28 *Ibid.*
29 Khrushchev, N., *Khrushchev Remembers*, Little Brown, Boston, 1970.
30 *Ibid.*
31 Kennedy, J., *John F. Kennedy: Words to Remember*, Hallmark, USA, 1967.
32 Cited in Fairley, P., *Man on the Moon*, Mayflower, London, 1969.
33 *Ibid.*
34 *Ibid.*
35 Nixon, R., *Setting the Course*, Funk & Wagnalls, New York, 1970.
36 Khrushchev, *op.cit.*
37 Cited in Kennedy, R., *13 Days*, Macmillan, London, 1969.
38 *Ibid.*
39 *Ibid.*
40 Smith, M., *UPI News Report*, 23 November 1963, United Press International.
41 Cited in Manchester, W., *Death of a President*, Michael Joseph, London, 1967.
42 *Ibid.*
43 Johnson, L.B., *The Vantage Point*, Weidenfeld & Nicolson, London, 1972.
44 *Time* magazine, 29 November 1963.
45 Cited in Baker, P., *Martin Luther King*, Wayland, London, 1974.
46 *Report of the National Advisory Commission on Civil Disorders*, US Government Printing Office, Washington DC, 1968.
47 Dylan, B., *Lyrics 1962–1985*, Jonathan Cape, 1987.
48 *Newsweek* magazine, 2 June 1969.
49 Furer, H. (ed.), *Lyndon Johnson Presidential Documents*, Oceana, New York, 1971.
50 *The Pentagon Papers*, New York Times Books, New York, 1971.
51 *New York Times*, 8 April 1965.
52 US Department of Defense.
53 *Ibid.*
54 US State Department.
55 Kennedy, R., *Apostle of Change*, Simon & Schuster, New York, 1968.
56 *Time* magazine, 3 January *1972.*
57 Nixon, *op.cit.*
58 *Newsweek* magazine, 5 February 1973.
59 Bailey and Kennedy, *op.cit.*
60 *Time* magazine, 3 January 1972.
61 *The White House Transcripts*, New York Times Books, New York, 1974.
62 University of Michigan Institute for Social Research, 1974.
63 *New York Times*, 9 August 1974.
64 Heren, L., *The Story of America*, Times Books, London, 1976.
65 Ford, G., *A Time to Heal*, W.H. Allen, London, 1979.
66 Carter, J., *Keeping Faith*, Collins, London, 1982.
67 Cooke, A., *America*, BBC Books, London, 1973.

Index

Figures in **bold** refer to illustrations.

racial discrimination 18–19, 59
  riots 34–5, **34**
Reagan, Ronald W. 49, 50–51, **50,** 55, 57
Roosevelt, Franklin D. 5, **5,** 6, 56

SALT treaties 45, 57
Second World War 6–7, 56
segregation 9, 14, 18–19, 56, 59
space exploration 15, 23, 26–7, 56
Star Wars 57
student protest 36–7, **37**

Truman, Harry S. 8–9, **9,** 55, **55,** 56
Truman Doctrine 10–11

USA
  civil disorders 34–7, **34**
  crime 38–9
  economy 4, 20–21, 51
  foreign policy 7, 10–11, 12–13,
    15, 22, 24–5, 44–5, 48,
  glasnost 50
  gun control laws 39
  health care 9, 21, 23
  industry 4, **4**

poverty 21
schools 18–19
space programme 26–7
stock market crash 4, 51
unemployment 5
USSR
  confrontation over Berlin 24–5
  glasnost 50
  human rights 48
  Nixon visit 43, 44, 45
  space programme 26
  strategic arms agreement 45, 57
  tension with USA 8, 10–11, 15,
    44–5, 50
United Nations 7, 8, 56

Vietnam War 23, 32–3, **41,** 44, 56, 57
  protests against **33,** 40–41, **40,**
    42
violence 37, 38–9
Voting Rights Act (1965) 34

Watergate scandal 43, 46–7, 57
women's movements 33, **36,** 37